HOSHINO'S ALASKA

HOSHINO'S ALASKA

MICHIO HOSHINO Foreword by Lynn Schooler Introduction by Karen Colligan-Taylor

CHRONICLE BOOKS

SAN FRANCISCO

ALEUTIAN ISLANDS

The following essays have been translated from the Japanese by Karen Colligan-Taylor for this book:

"People of the Whale" (p. 14), "Early Spring" (p. 54), "The Wolf That Stole a Camera" (p. 97),
and "Brant Geese Take a Gamble" (p. 142) from *Kaze no yo a monogatari* [A Story Like the Wind] (Shogakukan, 1991)
"Moose" (p. 55) from *Moose* (Heibonsha, 1988)
"Another Kind of Time" (p. 100), "A Culture of Wood" (p. 138), "Forget-me-nots" (p. 143),
and "The Traveling Tree" (p. 156) from *Tabi wo suru ki* [The Traveling Tree] (Bungei Shunju, 1995)
"The Eternal Present" (p. 101) from *Nagai tabi no tojou* [On A Long Journey] (Bungei Shunju, 1999)
"Of Forests, Glaciers, and Whales" (p. 101) from *Mori to hyoga to kujira* [Of Forests, Glaciers, and Whales] (Sekaibunkasha, 1996)
"Caribou" (p. 143) and "Landscape and Stories" (p. 158) from *Arasuka hikari to kaze* [Alaska: Light and Wind] (Fukuinkan Shoten, 1995)

Library of Congress Cataloging-in-Publication Data:

Hoshino, Michio, 1952–1996
  Hoshino's Alaska / Michio Hoshino ; foreword by Lynn Schooler ; Introduction by Karen Colligan-Taylor.
    p. cm.
  "Essays have been translated from the Japanese by Karen Colligan-Taylor for this book."
  ISBN-13: 978-0-8118-5651-5
  ISBN-10: 0-8118-5651-8
  1. Wildlife photography—Alaska. 2. Wilderness areas—Alaska—Pictorial works. I. Title.

TR729.W54H67 2007
779'.309798—dc22   2006028505

Printed in China by Everbest Printing Co., Ltd.

English translation: Karen Colligan-Taylor
Art direction and book design: Atsushi Takeda (Souvenir Design)
Editing and production: Rico Komanoya (ricorico)

Distributed in Canada by Raincoast Books
9050 Shaughnessy Street
Vancouver, British Columbia V6P 6E5

10 9 8 7 6 5 4 3 2 1

Chronicle Books LLC
680 Second Street
San Francisco, CA 94107
www.chroniclebooks.com

Table of Contents

Foreword

Michio Hoshino once told me that a good photograph must tell an entire story. And in an age when proficient photography has been made commonplace by digital wizardry, the images in this book assure me no technology will ever take the place of the master storyteller. It was not technical expertise that allowed Michio to capture things as ephemeral as the wind sweeping across a mountainside or the soft affection of a moose nuzzling at its newborn calf; it was the heart of the man behind the lens. This, above all, was what separated Michio's work from all others. After more than a decade and a half of guiding wildlife photographers through Alaska's wilderness, I am convinced that the primary determinant of the content and quality of any photographer's work is that person's character. So open this book to any page at random (or start at the front or the back if that is more in keeping with your own personality) and move slowly from one image to another, from the serene landscape of the Arctic to the fertile, dripping rainforests of Southeast Alaska, and you will be journeying in the company of a master storyteller, one who never failed to approach his subjects with respect, curiosity, and affection. While many of the photographers I have known seem to pursue full-frame, as-close-as-possible portraits of wildlife as their constant ideal, Michio's gift was often to place an animal against an immense and powerful background, in such a way as to make the animal seem small, thus instructing us on the animal's life and environment rather than presenting a demand that we admire him for his daring. The first approach probably tells us as much about a photographer's willingness to disturb an animal for the sake of a picture as it does the subject, whereas the second strikes me as an example of Michio's willingness to reduce his own presence in a landscape in order to demonstrate for us how an entire mountain or valley may be brought to life by a single moose or bear.

Humility such as this was but one of the traits that always made Michio's company a great pleasure during the years that I knew him. Over the course of the weeks and months that we traveled together, sharing cramped cabins, small boats, and wet tents, I never once saw him fail to place the well-being of others above his own — even when that "other" was a four-legged or feathered friend. And the closest I ever heard him come to a brag was when he once shyly mentioned an upcoming exhibit at the prestigious Carnegie Museum, after which he literally blushed when I told him how impressed I was by his accomplishment. In other words, ego never seemed to take up much space in his camera bag or to impose itself on his photography.

Shy without being diffident, he was nevertheless consistently open to people in a way that inspired trust in those with whom he crossed paths. My favorite memories of the man are not those of sharing the jaw-dropping thrill of watching humpback whales feed alongside our boat or the heady rush of having a grizzly settle down to nurse her cubs a few yards away (unforgettable as those experiences were) but of watching him quietly approach someone who might at first be reserved or even suspicious of his motives. Inevitably, within minutes that person would be treating Michio as if they were old friends. This and the memory of the evenings we spent quietly discussing life are among my most cherished memories of him. And by "life," I do not mean the circumstances and generalities of human life alone, but that force that is the inner mechanism of the universe — a force, Michio often said, that he found "very mysterious" but nonetheless managed to capture in his photos. Time after time, he reached out with his camera and caught the particular moment of a caribou ascending a snow-clad ridge, a bird regarding the chicks in its nest, or a flower aching into bloom, which serves to perfectly describe that being's place within the intricacies of its environment. Studied carefully, his photo of a wolf nestled into a copse of dried grass tells us clearly how the demands of that animal's life require a state of constant awareness, just as his photo of a polar bear rimed in shining frost demonstrates the perfection with which that species has adapted to its environment. More, he consistently managed to present these images in such a way as to awaken our own veneration for nature.

Such praise would come dangerously close to gushing were it not for the number of times anyone thumbing through the pages of this book will feel compelled to stop and ponder one of Michio's photos or simple, profound essays. But they are the work of a master storyteller, and if, as stated at the beginning of this foreword, a person's inner character determines the quality of one's work, then Michio's quiet grace and deep inner connection to his beloved Alaska are apparent throughout. We are fortunate he was with us long enough to amass this stunning work, but perhaps cheated because he no longer continues. In consolation, I, like many others who still grieve at his passing, will find bittersweet uplift in these images, for within them he has done no less than present us with a record of that great mystery, the story of Life.

— Lynn Schooler

Living in the Moment

Michio Hoshino knew Alaska better than most of us. For two decades he explored the state from the fiords of Southeast Alaska to the ice of the Bering Sea, capturing on film the lives of humpback and bowhead whales, grizzly and polar bears, moose and wolves. He followed the migrating Porcupine caribou herd, flowing like a living river across the Brooks Range and onto the coastal plain. He traveled with Native subsistence hunters and fishermen as they harvested the traditional foods that sustain their families and communities. On winter nights in the Alaska Range, he captured the dancing colors of the northern lights. Wherever he went, he made friends.

Appropriately, Michio's northern odyssey began with a photograph. One fall afternoon in 1972, while browsing through the used-book stores of Tokyo's Kanda district, Michio came across *Alaska*, published by the National Geographic Society. At that time books on Alaska were rare in Japan. Michio relates that he carried the book around everywhere in his knapsack as he commuted on Tokyo's trains. Thumbing through its pages, he was drawn to one particular photograph — an aerial view of the Inupiat island village of Shishmaref taken by George F. Mobley. Intrigued by this place that was no more than a dot within the vastness of Alaska, Michio determined that he would explore this landscape himself. Late that fall he wrote to seven Alaskan villages, but to whom should he address the letters? He decided on this format: Mayor, Shishmaref, Alaska, USA. Most of the letters were returned undelivered. Then, one spring day, there was a response from the very place that had so piqued his interest.

Shishmaref, Alaska 99772
April 11, 1973

Dear Mr. Hoshino,
Sorry for delay in answer. My wife and I have talked of your possibly to stay with us, but we must know what month you plan to be here.
Month of June and July we spend most of the time in the country tending my reindeer herd. I handle reindeer between July 10 and 15th to mark and dehorn reindeer.
If I know appropriate date you arrive here it would be helpful for me. Also I could arrange your travel from Nome to Shishmaref. You are welcome to stay with us.

Sincerely,
Clifford Weyioyanna

Originally Michio had planned to spend just two weeks in Shishmaref, but he kept asking to stay one more week, until, in the end, he had spent all three months of summer 1973 with the Weyioyannas, forming a deep bond with this four-generational Eskimo family.

After completing a degree in economics at Keio University in 1976, Michio began studying photography as an assistant to Japanese photographer Kojo Tanaka. Technical skill would not be enough, however. In 1978, he enrolled in an English program in Seattle, taking pictures during his free time in Olympic National Park. Michio was captivated by old-growth coastal forest. That fall he was admitted to the Fairbanks campus of the University of Alaska to take courses in wildlife biology. Fairbanks was to become his base camp as he journeyed through the state to photograph northern landscapes, people, and wildlife. In his journal of 1978 he writes: *I hope to draw a map of my personal experiences on top of the blank map of Alaska.*

In June 1979 he embarked on his first kayak trip in what is today designated Glacier Bay National Park and Preserve in Southeast Alaska. It was here that I first met Michio. He told me that he planned to spend about four weeks exploring both arms of the bay. In those days, Glacier Bay saw fewer kayakers than it does today. Until his final day, Michio did not encounter another person. He learned everything firsthand: how fast the waves approach one's kayak as a sheet of ice calves off a glacier; how to maneuver between icebergs; how far up the shore the tide will rise — despite my warning, he once had to swim for his kayak when it drifted off a beach; how frigid the water can be; how quickly the weather can change; and how important it is to bring more food than you think you will need. After three weeks he had nothing left but rice and soy sauce. This was a small price to pay for the opportunity to smell the breath of a humpback whale, find himself surrounded by a pod of orca, and learn how to photograph harbor seals with pups resting on the ice. He had to paddle ever so slowly, maintaining a respectful distance.

The day after his return, Michio stopped by for dinner. My husband, Mike, and I were building a cabin in the forest just outside the park. Electricity and phone service were many years in the future. Our kitchen was a lean-to frame with a plastic tarp; our water source a pitcher-pump; and our refrigerator, a hole in the ground. We have a commemorative picture of the three of us taken by Michio on that evening of nearly twenty-four-hour daylight in early July. He is not quite 27, deeply tanned, glowing with health and adventure. He is wearing a blue sweater, denim overalls, and the standard Southeastern rubber boots. His hair is thick and black, growing too long for its bowl-shaped cut. A comfortable smile lights up his rounded face. We were all at the beginning of our careers — I was completing my doctorate at Stanford, Mike was starting his first season as a park naturalist, and Michio was developing his portfolio as a professional photographer.

When I accepted a teaching position at the University of Alaska Fairbanks in 1984, Michio reentered our lives. His base camp in those days was a one-room rental cabin without water, but he frequently enjoyed Japanese home-cooking and a warm bath at the Fairbanks home of Shuko Nishiyama, whom he adopted as a second mother. Along his path to fame, Michio kept his friends laughing. One winter night he stepped out in underwear and bunny boots to use the outhouse and locked himself out of his cabin. Grabbing a sleeping bag from his car to wrap and warm his bare skin, Michio ran next door to borrow the phone and called Shuko to the rescue.

Whenever Michio had something exciting to share he would drop by unannounced. On January 16, 1986, he knocked on the door of our dilapidated faculty housing and proudly presented us with the Japanese edition of his first book of photographs: *Grizzly* (November 1985).

Tramping through the mountains of Alaska, I frequently encountered grizzlies. One spring day I spotted a grizzly sow and cub playing in the lingering snow. They were in the midst of a game of tag. When the cub ran away, the sow would pursue it. These actions were repeated many times, until the sow finally caught the cub. I burst out laughing at the scene that followed, as the mother

bear continued to play with her young. The sow firmly grasped the cub with two paws and rolled down the mountain slope, the cub in her arms.

As America was settled, there was little space left for the grizzly, but in Alaska one can still encounter the great bear on a spring hillside. (*Grizzly*, English edition, 1987)

Unlike many photographers who fly in, take a few pictures, and fly out, Michio took the time to know his subjects and become comfortable with them. Through long hours he gained the trust of a grizzly sow who eventually allowed him to join her and her cubs on a Denali hillside. "She was a generous bear," he would say. *Grizzly* was introduced by Frederick Dean, professor of wildlife biology at the University of Alaska, and Jay Hammond, governor of Alaska. In 1986 Michio won his first award in Japan, the Anima Prize for Wildlife Photography. He was earning a reputation in both Japan and Alaska.

Our careers were progressing. In August 1986 my husband and I built a home on Chena Ridge overlooking the Tanana River and the Alaska Range, and a few years later, captivated by our forest of white spruce, birch, and aspen, Michio bought the lot next door. Here he built the log home of his dreams and truly set down roots; it was to this home he would bring his bride, Naoko, and begin to raise a family.

Grizzly was followed by *Moose* in 1988, with an introduction by Catherine Attla, an Athabaskan elder from Huslia. Catherine recalls that when she went to meet a Japanese man who had expressed an interest in the moose hunt, the only person who got off the Cessna appeared to be an Alaska Native. (It was Michio!) In the many days they spent together Catherine told stories about her father, a shaman, and shared with Michio the traditional wisdom of her people.

The covenants that govern man's actions in the natural world: to whom or what, exactly, are these promises made? A moose is taken, eaten, and today a portion of it is returned to nature. This means that the spirit of the moose is returned to the forest. Now that this has been done, a moose may appear to the hunters once again.

As Catherine and Steven hung the hide from the moose head on an aspen branch, I recalled an Eskimo whale hunt in which I had once participated. When they had finished butchering the whale, the Eskimos pushed its giant jawbone back into the sea. As it slipped off the ice pack, the people called out for it to return again next year. To return the jawbone of the whale to the sea, to return the hide of the moose to the forest, is to assure that the circle will be unbroken. (Moose, 1988)

After *Moose*, each year saw the publication of new books of photography and essays, and in 1990 Michio was awarded the 15th Ihei Kimura Prize, the highest recognition for photographic art in Japan. His work appeared regularly in photo magazines in Japan, the United States, and Europe, and exhibitions of his work were held worldwide. He was featured in Japanese television documentaries.

In 1992, some twenty years after Michio was drawn to Alaska by a chance encounter with a used book, and with his own map of Alaska nearly filled in, Michio received a phone call from bush pilot Don Ross: "George Mobley from *National Geographic* is in town, and he would like to consult with you about photographing the caribou migration." Michio began driving toward Mobley's hotel, then suddenly did a U-turn and rushed home. Where had he heard that name? Looking through his bookshelves, Michio found the old picture book with Mobley's photo. Delighted at last to meet the elder photographer, Michio reflected on how a single picture could shape a lifetime.

Michio was born in Ichikawa-shi, Chiba, Japan, the first son and youngest child of Itsuma and Yachiyo Hoshino. His parents still treasure an essay Michio wrote in junior high, its simple prose reflecting a sense of aesthetics and a consciousness of time unusual in one so young.

This World

This evening I rode to Edo River on my bike. When I was in elementary school I used to come here about once every three days with my friends. We'd lie down in the grass and talk about all kinds of things. But, I've come only two or three times since entering junior high. It's been too long.

If I ride my bike really fast, I can get to Edo River from my house in about five minutes. The bluff gets closer and closer. I ride up in one breath and there it is — the grand Edo River on its leisurely course. A small boat is tied up on the grassy banks, nameless flowers scattered about it. An ordinary scene. I pedal my bike very slowly. A cold northern wind buffets my face. The red sun, on the verge of sinking.

The river, flowing slowly. Birds, flying through the sunset sky. Now in this moment, a part of this beautiful natural scene, I am happy.

Michio's Japanese biographer, Toshihide Kunimatsu, relates that Michio's father was not the type who pressed his children to get good grades in school or to pursue a particular profession. He simply watched over his two daughters and son, observing the directions they chose to take. At turning points in their education he would talk to them seriously and ask, "How are things going?" or "How are you feeling about life right now?" Michio's father wanted his children to have the choices he never had: Itsuma's youth was defined by events leading up to the Pacific War. When Michio was sixteen his father was the only family member who consented to his son's traveling alone through the United States for the summer. Michio left Yokohama harbor and arrived fifteen days later in Los Angeles. He was thrilled, he recalls, to disembark at a strange port with no one to meet him.

Two other family influences were his sister Kyoko, who went to work in Hokkaido and introduced him to northern Japan, and his grandmother, who lived with the family. Perhaps it was the example set by his parents' kindness and respect for his grandmother that made it easy for Michio to establish close friendships with Alaskan elders, both Native and non-Native.

Michio was able to earn the trust of others, believes Sean McGuire, a Fairbanks friend, because he was comfortable with silence. Just as he would wait patiently for the perfect configuration of light and subject when taking a photograph, Michio was as receptive to the pauses between words as to the words themselves, patiently allowing a story to take shape.

Understanding the communicative value of silence is not unrelated to understanding differing perceptions of time. Although Michio came from a society in which an apology is in order if a train enters a station a few seconds late, he understood that in the far north people do not make plans by the clock. He would often cite the example of a European film crew that visited a certain Inupiat Eskimo village to photograph a hunting scene. They set the time at ten o'clock the following morning. However, at ten their hosts showed no sign of preparing for a hunt. These people are lazy, grumbled the crew. "Obviously," Michio would explain, "that type of scheduling means nothing in the wilderness. Here people conduct their lives according to natural conditions and their own rhythm."

Michio was fond of the books of German writer Michael Ende

(1929 – 1995), particularly *Momo* (1973). A central theme in Ende's work is time. Ende holds in deep regard the "ever-present" of childhood and cautions us, as adults, to be mindful not to live at so fast a pace that we leave our hearts behind. This concept corresponds to the Japanese character *isogashii*, "to be busy." It is composed of two parts: "to lose" and "one's heart." Michio was also influenced by Japanese writers, including Kenji Miyazawa (1896 – 1933), who wove the natural history of his native Iwate Prefecture and his personal Buddhist view of life into remarkable children's tales.

Possessing a certain childlike innocence himself, Michio loved children. After he built his log home he began inviting a group of Japanese children each spring to camp out at Ruth Glacier under the northern lights in Denali National Park. He hoped that the brief escape from a fast-paced world of video games and cram school would provide an alternate vision. He began to write books for children, sharing his ideas about wild nature (*The Grizzly Family Book*, 1994), the food chain, the cycle of life, and another kind of time.

A recurring theme in Michio's work is the relationship of life to habitat. In one photograph, a lone grizzly is dwarfed by a mountain valley. Michio was fascinated by the expanse of land necessary to sustain a top predator. People are part of the landscape as well, and Michio often photographed their subsistence activities. His photo of an Athabaskan hunter hauling a bloody moose carcass home in a flat-bottomed riverboat met resistance from one American publishing company. The editor refused to use this scene because it might offend "nature lovers." Michio was astounded by such shortsightedness. "Life feeds on life," he said. "Why are some people unable to see the beauty in this natural process?" These ideas gave birth to his children's book, *Nanook's Gift* (1996).

Although Michio took tens of thousands of photographs to select only the most artistic for his published collections, the photograph was not his ultimate aim. His goal was pure experience, to live each moment with the greatest possible awareness and gratitude. In his opening statement for a 1993 exhibition at the Carnegie Museum of Natural History in Pittsburgh, Michio writes:

One summer morning north of the Brooks Range, an arctic fox ambled by my camp. Not long after, a grizzly bear and her cubs appeared, then vanished across the tundra. That afternoon caribou began to fill the distant horizon. What first seemed to be a group of fifty or sixty, swelled to a herd of hundreds, then thousands. As the great living wave approached, I realized I was in the migration path of the Porcupine herd, numbering one hundred thousand animals. I set up my tripod and aimed my camera. But, standing on the Arctic Refuge coastal plain, I could not take a picture that would encompass the whole procession. Finally I gave up, sat on the ground, and put away my equipment. A rising chorus of clicking hooves accompanied by grunts and bleats resonated across the tundra. As the animals approached, I listened intently, fixing the sight and sound in my memory....

There I sat, like a rock, as the ungulate river flowed around me. For a moment I was a small piece of the arctic tapestry.

Michio's photographs, essays, and experiences — all have a place in this arctic tapestry. On August 8, 1996, Michio was pulled from his tent and killed by a brown bear at Kurilskoya Lake, a remote wildlife refuge in southern Kamchatka, Russia. Just as there are all kinds of people, there are all kinds of bears.

At Michio's memorial services and in the stories written and told since, we have come to realize that people throughout Alaska and Japan felt they had their own special relationship with Michio. We recognize in all these tales his talent, perseverance, humor, and foibles — but are also intrigued by that personal element or set of experiences characterizing each friendship. Michio was wonderful at connecting people, and many of us have friendships we owe to him.

Some of Michio's ashes lie under a cairn along the Jago River in the Arctic National Wildlife Refuge. Sitting on those banks on an August afternoon, I recalled one of Michio's stories about the refuge. He is flying with Don Ross over the coastal plain in Don's Cessna 185 as the Porcupine caribou herd streams by below. "It's just as it was one thousand years ago, ten thousand years ago," observes Don. Under the low angle of the midnight sun, the tundra is gold. "But I wonder what this place will be like one hundred years from now?" muses Michio. "Whatever happens," says Don, "this moment is a gift."

— Karen Colligan-Taylor

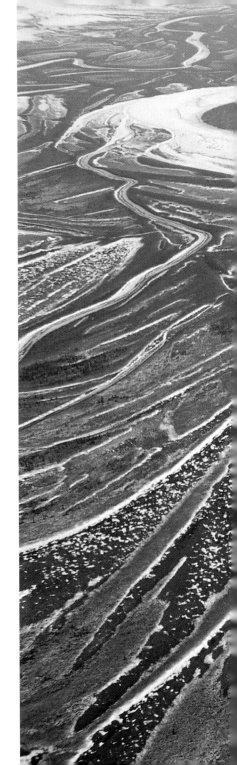

THE ARCTIC

People of the Whale

There is an instant in which human endeavor is transformed into art. On this bright summer night, white spray rises up from the Arctic Ocean, slowly getting closer and closer. Blowing as they touch the surface, bowhead whales make their way north. The whaling camp is veiled in silence. The Eskimo whalers camped on the shorefast ice all have their eyes fixed on a single whale, approaching unknowing of what destiny holds.

Umiaks (traditional Eskimo canoes made of skins of the bearded seal) stand ready to be pushed off at any moment. Now all wait silently.

The moon is full. The entire area is bathed in the pale white light of the summer night. The sea is completely calm. As carefully planned, ten or more umiaks slide in unison into the sea. Numerous silhouettes head silently through the glistening water toward a single point. These tiny human forms working so earnestly within the vastness of nature create a poignantly beautiful scene.

I return to my senses as I fall in with the group. The umiak is pushed off the ice with one heave, and before I know it I am paddling with six Eskimos. The paddles dip into the water at a frightful pace, and with difficulty I fall into the rhythm. Something my Eskimo friends have told me runs through my mind.

"All right, Michio? You head toward the whale and paddle for all you're worth. You can't splash. The whale would notice. You have to paddle silently with all your might."

There isn't any time to look at the whale. Although we are moving along at an incredible pace, the only sound is that of the paddles cutting into the water. My mouth is dry. I feel I have reached my limits.

"It's no good," one of the hunters shouts. We rest our paddles and I look ahead for the first time. A huge black mass moves quietly beyond our view, toward the jumbled ice. The only sound we hear among us is labored breathing. The umiak rocks gently in the quiet sea.

April 1982. Point Hope, an Eskimo village on the Arctic Ocean. This morning's whale hunt begins with a bowl of hot caribou soup. The caribou we shot on a hunt two weeks ago lies in front of me. In order to make soup we use an ax to hack meat from the frozen carcass. My job at camp is to help the women prepare meals. When I fill my mouth with fragments of meat that have scattered about, the icy bits thaw into a faint sweetness.

Around this time the ice that has covered the Bering Sea and the Arctic Ocean slowly begins to break and move. Due to the action of the wind and the currents, long fissures develop in the pack ice, revealing the ocean surface. This water is called a lead. Bowhead whales head toward the Arctic Ocean from the Bering Sea, following these leads. The leads permit the whales to surface and breathe.

Whaling camps are set up along these leads. Generally leads develop five to ten kilometers out from land. The lead must be the right width. If the lead is too narrow, even if it is possible to harpoon the whale, the animal may disappear under the ice before it dies. On the other hand, if the lead is too wide, a man-powered umiak cannot catch the whale.

This year the leads are quite unstable. Three weeks have passed since we set up whaling camp, and whaling season is nearing its end. This doesn't mean that the whales have all gone by. Until June a great many whales will pass through these waters. However, before that, the shorefast ice will melt away and the lead itself will deteriorate. If the lead disappears, one is face to face with the vast Arctic Ocean, making the pursuit of whales with an umiak impossible.

"What if we don't take even one." A feeling of unease begins to spread through the village. "What if we have to go through a whole year without being able to eat whale meat...." This is not the uneasiness of old, when people faced certain famine. Times have changed. All you have to do is peel out a few bills to have food brought in from the outside. But this is different. There is something that has to be preserved at all costs within our changing lives. Something that will continue to teach us who we are. For the Eskimo people, this is whaling, and it all depends on the lead.

THE INTERIOR
AND SOUTHWEST

Early Spring

Spring has at last arrived in Alaska, and today I will begin a long season of camping.

I spread out the tent that has been shut away all winter. On ground just exposed by melting snow, I connect the poles, thrust the pegs into the soil, and pull the tension lines tight. As I assemble the tent, I am reassembling my own feelings after the long winter.

Inside is the familiar smell of my old, well-used shelter. Last autumn's fallen leaves are still stuck in the corners. Rolling over on my back I pass my eyes over the rest of the tent. It's pretty worn and ripped up, but it'll probably hold out for one or two more years.

Last fall it was tested. One autumn morning I was awakened by the shaking tent and looked up to see what was going on. A bear's paw was silhouetted against the ceiling, lit up by the morning sun. I sat up and instinctively slapped the paw off the tent. I heard the bear lope away, and only then did I begin to experience fear. It's true we were separated by a few millimeters of cloth and that I couldn't see its face, but I had actually slapped a bear's paw! I can still recall how it felt. The bear must have been just as startled. After all, it was simply touching the tent out of curiosity.

The Steller's jay, alighting on a spruce branch, is an early arrival. After a brief rest it circles down to land on my pack. Perhaps this camp robber is delighting in finding its first guest of the season. It's all right. When all the other birds have migrated south, you remain with us in Alaska. I'm happy to celebrate the advent of spring with you.

The bright bird contrasts with my faded pack. I bought it the first year I arrived in Alaska. I still remember asking the owner of the camping goods store, "Is this the largest pack sold in the United States?" I somehow felt that since I would need to take long trips, I had to have the largest possible pack. Now my worn pack looks somehow very small. Twelve years have gone by.

I go to the river to fetch water. There is no more telling sound of spring than that of a river rushing with snowmelt. I wonder if this is the same sound that flows through the boughs of birch trees, leafed out in fresh green. They say that if you put your ear to the trunk and listen carefully, you can hear the sound of the water being sucked up from the ground by the roots. What constitutes this incredible strength?

Spring's first migrant, the black-bellied plover, flits about the riverbank. Perhaps it has begun to build its nest. Everything is just the same as it was last year. Naturally. Everything is repeated in an endless cycle, indifferent to human joy and sorrow. Perhaps this is why we find solace in the predictable order of nature's progression.

I fill the camp pot with water and wash my rice. The bottom of the pot is warped and bumpy, but I can't bring myself to throw it away. Pursuing caribou in the Alaskan Arctic, kayaking through Glacier Bay, waiting for the aurora in the Alaska Range. It was this pot that cooked my rice wherever I went. It is filled with as many memories as the dents and bumps on the bottom.

I wash my face and moisten my throat. Taking off my shoes, I soak my feet in the river. These hiking boots are the single new addition to my worn equipment. It will take a while for my feet to get used to them, but this in itself will prolong the feeling of newness.

I lie down on the riverbank, still damp from snowmelt, inhaling the fragrant earth of early spring. Wild crocus have sent up their pale purple buds. As I vacantly watch the clouds in the soft light, I become painfully aware of the sound of my heartbeat.

It's moments like this that make me want to call out, "Hey there, Time. I wish we could meet again, just as I knew you during my childhood."

I walk through the evening spruce forest, gathering dry twigs. The damp air is smooth and warm. The moose droppings lying on the forest carpet have absorbed some of this moisture. New willow shoots have sprouted. From here and there I hear the chatter of a red squirrel. The forest, too, has begun to stir.

Flames flicker in my small fire. The fire's crackling, *pachi pachi, pachi pachi,* relaxes my mind. Now, to sit here and sip hot coffee — what more could I possibly need?

How strange, human emotions. We're pushed left and right by the petty details of our everyday lives, when we could be enriched by no more than a pair of new hiking boots and the visages of spring.

Night falls, and the stars emerge. I light my lantern and begin writing in my journal. A new field season has begun.

Moose

A deep relationship exists between the moose and the Athabaskan Indian. The meat that is taken from the giant animal provides food during the long winter. Clothes made from moose hide protect people from the winter cold. At one time a variety of tools and ornaments were made from the bones and the lining of the stomach and other organs. In those days, the capture of a moose must have represented an even greater joy than it does today.

Moose hunting season had passed and winter drew near. One day, Catherine and Steven said that they were going to the forest to return the hide from the moose's head.

"Why are you going to do this?" I asked, walking along with them. The world seemed to be dyed a dazzling yellow, as light poured down between the clouds through branches of aspen.

"Because this is what we have always done," replied Steven.

"You have to return the skin from the head to the forest. If you don't, your luck will turn bad," Catherine continued. The cool air of late autumn felt good, and we could smell the scent of the forest.

The covenants that govern man's actions in the natural world: to whom or what, exactly, are these promises made? A moose is taken, eaten, and today a portion of it is returned to nature. This means that the spirit of the moose is returned to the forest. Now that this has been done, a moose may appear to the hunters once again.

As Catherine and Steven hung the hide from an aspen branch, I recalled an Eskimo whale hunt in which I had once participated. When they had finished butchering the whale, the Eskimos pushed its giant jawbone back into the sea. As it slipped off the icepack, the people called out for it to return again next year.

To return the jawbone of the whale to the sea, to return the hide of the moose to the forest, is to assure that the circle will be unbroken.

The Wolf That Stole a Camera

It was one of those bright white nights of early summer.

I was camped at Stony Hill, facing Mt. McKinley. It must have been close to eleven p.m. I had just finished photographing the mountain and was brewing a pot of coffee.

On these white northern nights, the flow of time seems to stand still. The sun, barely drifting below the horizon, makes no clear distinction between day and night. One can read in the twilight, and the stars are never visible.

I looked up to find a wolf standing right before me, staring at me intently. Wolves are normally secretive, conducting their lives deep in the wilderness, but this one was only five or six meters away.

Behind the wolf, the peak of Mt. McKinley was still lit by a faint afterglow. Without quite believing my eyes, I began to take pictures. While I changed film, I set one of my cameras down on the ground.

Just then the wolf suddenly stepped forward, grabbed the camera strap, and took off with it. It's not that the wolf was fleeing. It was simply trotting along at a leisurely pace. For a moment I could only watch in blank amazement at this wolf hauling off my camera.

The strap was long, and my camera, dangling at the end, bumped along the uneven terrain. Surely he'll just drop it, I thought, but the wolf headed on without pause. He showed no sign of stopping. It was the new camera I had just bought this year.

Suddenly I began running. I had to get it back. What did the wolf plan to do with my camera, anyway?

The wolf started running too. As I pursued the wolf, thinking what a stupid, deplorable situation this was, I began to tire. How far was I going to have to run, anyway?

My foot caught in a patch of lingering snow, and I almost fell. When I glanced up again, the wolf, now running at full speed, was no longer carrying anything.

I found my camera where he had dropped it in the snow. Brushing off the icy granules, I picked it up carefully. Was it broken?

At any rate, I felt relieved to have it back.

The coffee had boiled down, and the afterglow on McKinley's summit had vanished. Soon it would be dawn. The sun would rise two hours after it had dipped below the northern horizon. I sipped the bitter brew as a chilly breeze swept through my campsite under the pale sky.

I'm still using that camera. Now and then I think about that unusual night, and I wonder again what got into that wolf's head.

All I know is that among all my equipment, that particular camera carries with it a special tale.

THE SOUTHEAST COAST

Another Kind of Time

During my childhood I was strongly drawn to the natural world of Hokkaido. At that time Hokkaido seemed to me to be a very distant place. As I read many books, one image began to catch my attention. Grizzlies. When I was jostled back and forth by the trains of the great metropolis of Tokyo, or buffeted about by waves of human congestion, the grizzlies of Hokkaido would suddenly appear in my mind. At the same instant I was living in Tokyo, in this same country, Japan, grizzlies were breathing, conducting their daily lives. At this very moment on some mountain a lone grizzly was trudging ahead, making its way over a fallen tree. This contrast struck me as indescribably strange. It was the wondrous realization that time flows by equally for all things.

A few years ago a friend of mine said something quite similar. Somehow making arrangements to leave her busy job as an editor in Tokyo, she accompanied me for one week on a trip to photograph whales in Southeast Alaska.

One evening we came upon a group of humpback whales. As they drew near, blowing, we slowly approached them in our small boat. We were so close, that their heavy breath seemed to settle on our heads. Around us was a landscape of glaciers and old-growth forest, and in this eternal flow of time all elements of nature breathed in harmony.

Suddenly one of the whales leaped up from the water just before our eyes. Dancing up toward the sky, it seemed to hover in space for just an instant, before slowly descending and crashing back into the sea. It was a solemn image — almost like something you would see on film in slow motion.

The sea quieted and the whales advanced powerfully as if nothing had happened. I've seen this kind of behavior, called breaching, any number of times, but this is the closest I have ever been to a breaching whale. People try to provide explanations for every type of animal behavior, but in the last analysis, how can we really know what the whales are trying to convey? Perhaps this whale simply wanted to feel the wind, to leap up just for the fun of it.

My friend was rendered speechless. What had moved her so deeply was not the huge body of the whale that filled the camera frame, but the vastness of nature that encompassed this scene. It was the smallness of the whales that lived in that vast world. It was, however brief, that one instant of time that she shared with the whales. Many months later, she spoke of her experience. "Although I was busy with my work in Tokyo, I'm truly glad that I went. What was so rewarding? The realization that while I am working frantically in Tokyo, in that same instant, a whale may be breaching in the waters of Southeast Alaska."

There is no doubt that as we live each second of our lives, another kind of time flows by on its leisurely course. A constant awareness of this parallel time, tucked in some corner of our hearts or minds, can make a vast difference in our perception of life.

The Eternal Present

The other day I was floating down an Alaskan river in a rubber raft. Entrusting myself to the current, I suddenly noticed that in a cottonwood along the riverbank ahead of me perched a bald eagle. As the current pulled the boat rapidly toward the tree, I could see the eagle staring down at me intently. I watched the eagle casually, wondering if it would fly off or allow me to pass right under it. There followed a moment of tension, in which I almost dared not breathe. For the bald eagle that stared down at me, there was neither past nor present, simply an encounter with each new second. I, too, focused on the immediate present, as I had in those distant days of childhood. This was a point in time that did not allow for any distinction between me and the eagle; it was an eternity in the present. I found myself drawn into its empty depths. The eagle remained motionless as my raft passed beneath the cottonwood.

Of Forests, Glaciers, and Whales

As I look at the coastal mountains, I see that each valley was once filled with a glacier. The glaciers that had covered the land are slowly retreating. Eventually forests will take form on deglaciated gravels and whales will return to the deep fiords. How many times have these processes been repeated during our earth's history? I was overcome with the feeling that forests, glaciers, and whales were closely bound on this eternal voyage through time.

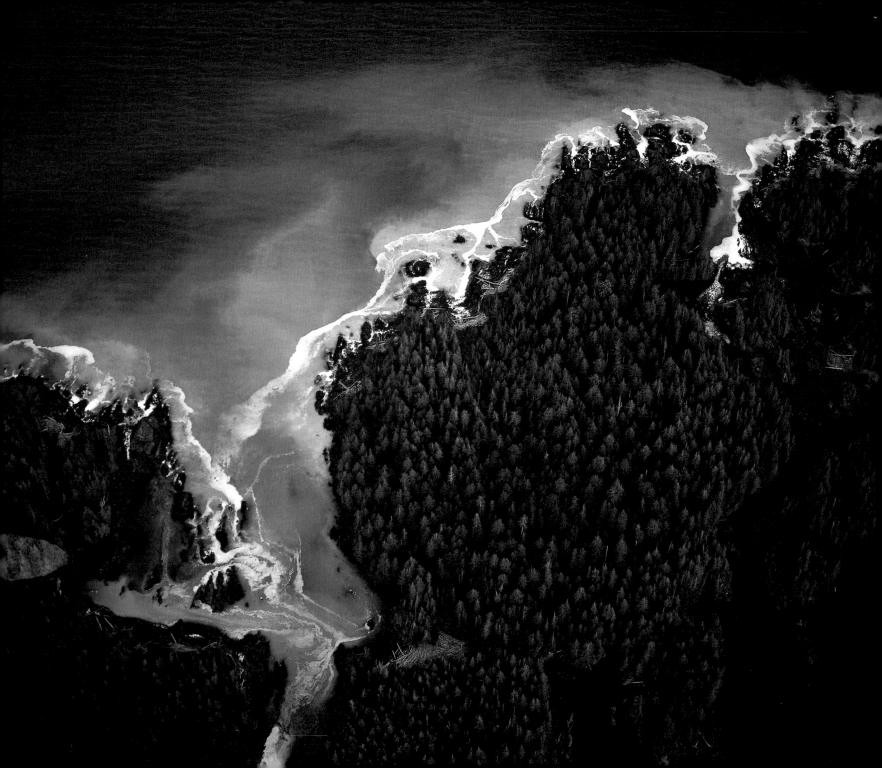

A Culture of Wood

Bald Eagle, Raven, Whale, Bear ... these mysterious designs hold the memories of Haida and Tlingit ancestors and myths. These are not products of a culture of stone, whose monuments will remain in the distant future, but records left by a culture of wood, subject to natural processes of decay.

Along the Northwest coast today, it is easy to find Indian villages with decorative totem poles. But the villagers' lifestyle has changed dramatically. Even if today's poles bear the same designs as those of the past, they do not speak to us in the manner of their prototypes. This is because the old tales no longer live in the heart of the carver. Whale and Bear and Eagle have been left somewhere in the passage of time.

I had always wanted to see the old poles, and then one day I heard about a place in the Queen Charlotte Islands. Europeans had brought smallpox to this isolated region, killing over seventy percent of the six thousand villagers, and compelling those who survived to abandon their homes and establish a new life elsewhere.

In the twentieth century large museums from all over the developed world sought out art objects of historical relevance. The Queen Charlotte Islands did not go unnoticed, and many totem poles were removed. Eventually the descendants of the Haida decided that it was best to leave their sacred places and artifacts to decay naturally. They began to oppose outside pressure to remove the poles.

Evidence of human life on these islands takes us back seven thousand years. But in less than fifty years from now these last totem poles, born in the age of myth, will disappear in the forest. The dream-like tales chiseled in these poles — one can hardly distinguish whether they are tales of humans or animals — were created instinctively of man's relationship to nature and constituted the wisdom that sustained this culture. At the same time, they represent a certain power, now lost to us.

NORTH
TO THE ARCTIC

Brant Geese Take a Gamble

For how many years, I wonder, did I search for snowy owls each spring on the Arctic tundra? I yearned to photograph this white northern owl.

The locations and nesting habits of the snowy owl may shift according to the abundance of its primary prey, the lemming. Lemming populations rise and fall in cycles; when the lemming population is low, the snowy owl will not build a nest.

Finally, in June 1988 I discovered the nest of a snowy owl in the basin of the Colville River, near the Arctic Ocean. This creature I had longed to meet had laid four eggs alongside a nondescript hillock, about 30 centimeters high, on the tundra. I encountered the site quite by accident when I flushed the parent off the nest. I realized that I needed to leave immediately. The eggs would get cool if I kept the adult away.

Suddenly I felt a heavy thump on my back and lost my balance. No sooner had the large wings before me circled upward than the bird changed its direction and headed down again straight toward me. The owl's large yellow eyes were fixed on me. Dodging this second attack, I hurried away. When I reached my hand up under my sweater to feel my back, my fingers came out covered with blood.

A week later I constructed a blind near the nest and began photographing. On the flat tundra only my blind projected upward from the ground. I hoped the birds would somehow get used to it. At first the adult owl crouched down in the nest glared out at me, but gradually it regained its composure.

Arctic summers are hot. After sitting all day in a blind of one and a half square meters, my T-shirt was heavy with sweat. The mosquitoes seemed to arrive in an endless swarm. I must have smashed at least 200 mosquitoes each day.

One day as I looked through my binoculars, I could hardly believe my eyes. Aren't those black brants, building a nest of their own within thirty meters of the snowy owl nest? I asked myself.

Snowy owls are birds of prey with sharp talons, as I had experienced, and a powerful grip. If the number of lemmings is down, the owl will mercilessly invade the brant's nest. Not only are the adult geese unable to defend the chicks, they are easy prey themselves.

This being the case, why would the brants build their nest so close to the snowy owl?

The brant must know full well that she is laying her eggs near a snowy owl nest. Snowy owls begin building their nests well in advance of the geese.

Arctic foxes?

This image popped into my head. In the spring the Arctic tundra is a valuable breeding ground for migrating birds. At the same time, it is also heaven for arctic foxes, which eat eggs. A single fox may destroy an indeterminate number of nests.

It was different with the snowy owl's nest. The small arctic fox would be chased away by the owl. No doubt an animal that had once experienced such a pursuit would stay away from an owl nest.

Perhaps the brant geese "decided" to take a gamble. Rather than risk having their eggs taken by the arctic fox, they chose to take their chances with the snowy owl.

Nature sometimes allows us to read a story in the landscape. Landscapes through which we walk are full of stories. It's just that usually we don't know how to read them.

On July 12, the brant chicks hatched, and several days later all the chicks left the nest with the parent geese. Shortly afterward, the four snowy owl chicks also fledged their nest safely. Two empty nests remained on the tundra as the short Arctic summer drew toward its end.

The snowy owls hadn't attacked the geese, even though it wasn't a particularly high lemming year. Had the brant geese played this hand deliberately?

Forget-me-nots

A number of years ago I noticed clusters of forget-me-nots, the Alaska state flower, growing at our base camp along the coast of the Arctic Ocean. They quietly opened their pale blue petals, indifferent to the fact that they might not be seen in this remote spot.

At that time I was accompanied by a television crew who were filming a nature program. For a number of reasons the filming was progressing slowly, while the days went racing by. I understood only too well their anxiety about completing this program, but everyone was so consumed with this worry that I felt they weren't really seeing nature at all. This tense atmosphere began to concern me, and I decided to take the director aside for a chat: "Look, you've done your best," I told him, "but your subject is nature, so you can't expect everything to go as you plan. When you look back at this experience ten or twenty years later, it probably won't matter a great deal whether you were able to get excellent footage for this program or not. Rather than spending all your time fretting about the quality of the footage, wouldn't it be worthwhile to put aside a little time each day — even just fifteen or thirty minutes — to forget your work and observe closely that flowers are blooming, the wind is blowing, that you are camping on the edge of the vast Arctic Ocean. After all, this isn't the kind of place you can come to anytime, and it would be a shame to let this experience go by unnoticed."

I felt that the forget-me-nots nodding in the breeze were saying the same thing — that the time we can live is not in the past, not in the future, but right now in the present. Even if the result of the filming was not what we originally envisioned, the time we spent in this place was real. And, the ultimate meaning of our experience lay not in the result, but in that valuable segment of time during which we lived in this spot.

The touch of the Arctic wind caressing my cheeks, the sweet smell of the Arctic tundra, the pale light of these summer nights, clusters of forget-me-nots, so small as to be easily overlooked — I want to stand still, compose myself, and record this landscape in the memory of my five senses. I want to value these moments that flow by, without producing anything at all. I always want to know in my heart that there is another kind of time flowing by in parallel with the hectic conduct of man's daily life.

Caribou

There is an old saying among Native people of the far north: "No one knows where the wind or the caribou go." Although the great herds of caribou seem to cover the land even today as we enter the twenty-first century, there are few to watch their progress. Even if some lucky fellow were to encounter those great legendary herds in the wilderness, the next day there probably would not be a single caribou in sight on the entire tundra.

I'll never forget the day I became that lucky man. One summer afternoon the few caribou I saw as small dots in the distance, suddenly multiplied, becoming tens, then hundreds, then thousands of caribou filling the horizon. They were heading straight toward me. Soon I found myself in the center of tens of thousands of caribou. I felt taken back to an earlier page in the history of the earth. As I watched the river of animals disappear over the horizon, I was not only profoundly moved, but strangely saddened, as if I had just witnessed the passing of an age.

The Traveling Tree

If you travel along Alaska's rivers, you will encounter one of the symbolic landscapes of this region. In this flat landscape the river changes its course as it erodes the earth, little by little, over the long course of months and years. The trees within the forest will take their turn standing at the river's edge, ultimately falling over. The undercut forest tilts, then dips into the current, the tree branches sweeping the flowing surface of the stream. Some of the trees look as if they could take off downstream at any moment. I love these chaotic landscapes, shaped by the force of nature that cannot be arrested by the hand of man. Such scenes speak to me quietly of the truth that nothing stands still, that all things are moving constantly.

I remember one day, a long time ago, on my first visit to the coast of the Arctic Ocean, when I tried to take a picture of a single thrush, resting on the top of a beached log. I had found it odd that here, in the midst of the treeless Arctic tundra, a drifting tree would have been lifted up onto the shore. This was a spruce tree that had drifted down a river, and after a long journey had arrived at the sea. Carried along by an ocean current, it one day reached these distant northern shores. Its branches fallen off, and its bark peeled free, the tree had become implanted in the sand pointing up toward the sky. It had become a landmark, and not only provided a place for the thrush to rest its wings, but also a scent station where the arctic fox marks its territory. As it slowly rotted, it imparted nutrients to the soil, which one day might nourish flowers in their short summer bloom.

As I thought about this, the boundary between life and death became blurred, and I realized that all things have embarked upon an unending journey....

Major Works, Awards, Exhibitions

Major Works

*Photography Collections

Grizzly

Moose

Arasuka kyokuhoku seimei no chizu [Alaska: A Map of Life in the Far North]

Arasuka kaze no yo na monogatari [Alaska: A Story Like the Wind]

Arctic Odyssey

Hoshino Michio no shigoto [The Work of Hoshino Michio, 4 volumes]

*Essay Collections

Arasuka hikari to kaze [Alaska: Light and Wind]

Inyunikku seimci [Lifc]

Tabi wo suru ki [The Traveling Tree]

Mori to hyoga to kujira [Of Forests, Glaciers, and Whales]

Northern Lights

Nagai tabi no tojou [On a Long Journey]

Hoshino Michio chosakushuu [A Collection of Writing by Michio Hoshino; 5 volumes]

*Picture Books for Children

Arasuka tankenki [A Record of My Adventures in Alaska]

The Grizzly Bear Family Book

Mori e [Into the Woods]

Nanuuku no okurimono [Nanook's Gift]

Kuma yo [Hey, Bear]

Major Photography Awards and Exhibitions

1986 Third Anima Award for *Grizzly,* Third Anima Award Photo Exhibit, Old Olympus Gallery, Tokyo

1990 Arasuka *kyokuhoku seimei no chizu,* Old Olympus Gallery; later shown in Sapporo and other location

Fifteenth Kimura Ihei Prize for *Araska kaze no you na monogatari*

1991 *Arasuka kaze no yo na monogatari,* Old Olympus Gallery; later shown in Sapporo

1993 *Alaskan Tapestry,* Carnegie Museum of Natural History, Pittsburgh

1998 – 2000 *Hoshino Michio no sekai* [Michio Hoshino's World], Ginza Matsuya, Tokyo; later shown in 17 locations throughout Japan, including Yokohama and Osaka

Special prize of the Japanese photography Association

2003 – 2005 *Hoshino Michio no uchu* [Michio Hoshino's Universe], Ginza Matsuya, Tokyo; later shown in 14 other locations

The unexplored wilderness ... this had been my vision of the land.
But now, I was to see it in a new way. I began to feel that if I were to
pursue those people who are now fading away, persuade them to stop
and look back for a minute, and listen carefully to their words, that the
landscape would have many different stories to tell.

— Michio Hoshino

Acknowledgments

I am very pleased to see this English-language edition of my husband's photography and essays. In Japan we have seen publication of numerous editions of his photography and essay collections, but few works have appeared in English.

My husband did not go to Alaska to become a photographer. Rather, it was because of his deep attraction to Alaska and his desire to interact intimately with its landscape, wildlife, and people that he chose this path. It seems that his initial intent was to photograph Alaska for about five years, and then move on to another theme. However, as he lugged his heavy camera equipment and rucksack through the wilderness, spending nearly half of each year in his tent, five years went by in no time. Looking back at his work, he felt that he was still at the entrance to the Great Land. He became ever more deeply acquainted with its geography, climate, and wildlife and with the lives of Native peoples, who are such an integral part of this land and its history. As he looked at the life around him and reflected on the meaning of his own life, he continued to record what he saw and felt in photographs and words. Before long, he decided to settle permanently in Alaska. Viewing Alaska, not as a traveler or visitor, but as a resident, his feelings for the state deepened and this place became his lifelong theme.

I believe that Michio's thoughts will be well conveyed to his readers by the translations of his longtime friend and fellow Alaskan, Karen Colligan-Taylor. I'm very happy that both Karen and Lynn Schooler, Michio's guide on a number of trips in Southeast Alaska, were willing to share their thoughts and memories about my husband and his work.

Thanks to the help of his many Alaskan friends, Michio was able to pursue his photography in this vast, wild place. It is to all these friends that I dedicate this book, with my deepest gratitude.

— Naoko Hoshino

About the Authors

Michio Hoshino was born in 1952 in Ichikawa-shi, Chiba, Japan. In 1969 he sailed to Los Angeles on the *Argentina-maru* and traveled alone for two months across the United States. In 1973 he spent the summer with an Eskimo family in Shishmaref, Alaska. After graduating from the Faculty of Economics at Keio University in 1976, Michio worked as an assistant for photographer Kojo Tanaka for the next two years. He then enrolled in the Wildlife Management program at the University of Alaska Fairbanks, where he studied for four years. Using Fairbanks as his base camp, Michio took photographs of the natural scenery, wildlife, and people of Alaska. His photographs were published in national magazines, including *Audubon* and *National Geographic*. Michio was killed by a brown bear at Lake Kurilskoya on the Kamchatka Peninsula, Russia, while on a photography trip in 1996.

Lynn Schooler is a writer, wilderness guide, and photographer living in Alaska. His first book, an account of his friendship with Michio titled *The Blue Bear,* has been published in fourteen languages. He has been awarded the French literary prize *Prix trente millions d'amis* and won the *National Wildlife* grand prize for his photography.

Karen Colligan-Taylor grew up in the suburbs of Tokyo. She earned her Ph.D. in Japanese literature at Stanford University and founded Japanese language and culture programs at Whitman College and the University of Alaska. She is professor emerita, Japanese Studies, at the University of Alaska Fairbanks. Her publications in Japanese and English span topics in environmental literature, nature protection, and Japanese social issues.